Chicken Back Gravy and Such Delights: Life Lessons from my Journey

For my Beloveds, Mama and Bertland
And My Chicken Back Gravy Massive
We rise, we fall, and we rise again. Ever stronger.

Chicken Back Gravy and Such Delights: Life Lessons from my Journey

Professor Donna P. Hope

First published in Jamaica 2019 by

Donna P. Hope

Email: dqueen13@hotmail.com

ISBN: 978-976-96227-0-8 (paperback)

ISBN: 978-976-96227-1-5 (Kindle)

Cover and book design by Bertland Hope.

bertlandhope@icloud.com

Contents

Some Thoughts

After appearing on the Jamaican television show Profile with Ian Boyne (now deceased — RIP my dearest Friend) for the second time on Sunday, March 24, 2013 and receiving overwhelming responses to the snippet of my story that I shared then, I decided it was time to write a motivational book. And so I began. *Chicken Back Gravy and Such Delights* was born. I laid out my ideas and began writing. But life has a way of intervening. At that time I was a Head of Department at the University of the West Indies, Mona Campus and dealing with a raft of professional demands and challenges. I was also simultaneously tackling major challenges in my personal life, some of which will come out in one of my upcoming motivational works. My academic writing was also in the mix as I was finalizing my *Reggae from Yaad* collection and writing other academic articles for journals. With all these pressures my personal, motivational collection which I had long promised to deliver, was put on hold.

On New Year's Day, Sunday, January 1, 2017 sometime after 2pm, I met a policeman. A Constable. I was travelling along the Caymanas leg of the toll road from Kingston on my way to visit my family in Linstead. This was a chance meeting, the kind that occurs when you are speeding and you get caught in a speed trap. I ended up having a long conversation with this Constable and told him a bit about myself, some of my life's journey. Because he was curious. Most people are curious about me when we first meet. So I told him that I was a high school dropout at 15. A single teenage mother. From a poor family. Very poor at points. Scraping the bottom. He was struck by that wide disparity in my story. This man, this Constable, told me that he had been in the Jamaica Constabulary Force for more than twenty (20) years and had not been promoted since entering. He told me of his frustration, his desires, his hopes, his plans. We spoke at length in this chance meeting. One thing he said to me stuck with me. Something I had never thought about before. He said: "You must have had some luck to reach where you are now". This was a bit offensive to me. NO. I had worked damn hard to get here. This point has always been my mantra. But we spoke some more and I left that conversation on New Year's day in January 2017 with one gem that I must share. There is always some LUCK. You just have to see it. For a great segment of my life, Mama was my LUCK. I never thought about it that way until then. Life is always a learning experience. Without my mother's ever-present support and her constant motivation, I would not be the person I am today. She stood in the gap so I could go through. She did. Mama was my LUCK. Without her I could not and would not have taken such dangerous risks with my life, my time and my labour to win at this game. I would not have been able to do so because I would have been swamped in the backwater that constantly dragged at my every move. And so, again it came to me most forcefully, sitting in my vehicle on the Caymanas Toll Road on New Year's Day 2017, that I had a responsibility to share my fantastic Jamaican journey with others. This is something I have done intermittently in various talks, conversations and casually thrown statements over the years. This is something that my Son has constantly insisted on. So I went back to writing in January 2017. And then I left this project lying half complete. My ever-present Facebook family, people like Natalie Bartley and Garfield Goulbourne who have supported my every move, ask about *Chicken Back Gravy* intermittently. "I'm still working on it" I reply. I had been. In my head. Writing always occurs first in one's mind. But I put nothing on paper. Life rushed in.

Two things jarred me out of my reverie and pushed me to complete the manuscript for this first volume in June 2018. I was in my office at UWI on the Mona Campus doing three video shoots (*Business Access TV*, *Dancehall Documentary* and *LOOP News*) on Tuesday, June 19, 2018. After my second shoot with Jessica for her *Dancehall Documentary* we needed a photographer so we could both be in a few photographs for

Instagram and Facebook. And so I met Richard, a young UWI student passing by my door on the corridor, who became our willing photographer. Richard seemed a very responsive young man and, as we say in Jamaica, "very mannersable". He took the photos with both of our phones, we thanked him, and he left. Richard returned shortly after, when I was alone, knocking on my half-opened door. He needed my help with a document. And in the process of telling me about himself, he said that he read motivational books and biographies. He spoke about Marcus Garvey's works, Malcolm X's autobiography and motivational writers and works from the USA. "No" he said, "he could not find any Jamaican motivational writers". I felt bad. My works should have already been out there to be part and parcel of what could fill the gap for young people like Richard.

And then I went to see the screening of the documentary *Last Street* at Carib Cinema in Kingston on Monday, June 25, 2018. This was a documentary about at-risk young men (and women) in an inner-city community and their efforts to transform their lives. I knew the young men and women on that silver screen. I have lived those lives, walked those streets and sat in those places. I have held those hands and shared those stories along my life's variegated journey. The image of the pleasant and plump young woman, affectionately called Boom Boom, combing her 96-year old grandmother's hair, sitting at the doorway of a room that I knew from my early life moved me. The words "We are still here" whispered insistently through my head. I cried in Carib Cinema sitting between Rev. Ronnie Thwaites and my friend and colleague Dr. Lisa Tomlinson, with my Son one seat away and my mentee Shamar sitting in the row just ahead of us. After the screening I asked pointed questions. "What do you want to achieve from this documentary?" I took photos with the young men from Denham Town. We spoke. I whispered in a few ears. My heart ached. We spoke about *Last Street* for several days. I can see those images very clearly. Poor youths, locked away in the inner cities. Hoping to make it out. Somehow. There are so many voices that have been stilled. So many that have been left behind in those cages of poverty. I escaped.

I claim all these stories as mine because I have lived them and have lived the lives of others hundreds of times over. Everyone needs a story to which they can relate. I am a fortunate woman to have the privilege of reading and listened to many stories but also to have lived my own fascinating story and to have carved out a pathway through blood, sweat and a whole lot of tears. And so, this is one part of my present which I give to you. This first volume fills a vacuum. There is a yawning vacuum in the tidal wave of life coaches, motivational speakers and related parties whose words and suggestions have begun to grace our doorsteps here in Jamaica, but also, all over the world. I've always wanted to hear some stories that resonate with ME.

With YOU. With WHO we ARE. Who we HAVE BEEN. And who we are BECOMING. These are too few and far between. Even with those who are from similar backgrounds, I am concerned that many just parrot tried and tested mantras from highly developed societies where poverty looks different, lives in different locales and speaks in different tongues. Is it that there are no relatable success stories that speak in the language of poverty from my shores? Is there a meagre trickle? For black people? Africans in the diaspora? From my Yaad? From Jamaica? For Jamaicans? Well, here is the first volume of that *Chicken Back Gravy* Story that I promised you, complete with some Life Lessons and useful tips. It is MyStory.

Why Chicken Back Gravy?

Dinner tonight?,…Maybe
Same routine, Chicken Back Gravy
Bugle, *What We Gonna Do*, 2007

So many people ask me "Why *Chicken Back Gravy*"? Interesting name, but why? Let me explain. In every country there is a meal or dish associated with the poorest of the poor. In my country, my Yaad, Jamaica, during my childhood, and particularly during my turbulent teenage years in the 1980s, chicken back was the steak of the poorest, worst off citizens, those at the bottom of the social and economic ladder. These are usually the darker-skinned majority, those direct descendants of the African slaves who came here during plantation slavery. The closest Jamaican companion to Chicken Back at that time, Dutty Gyal (Dirty Girl) is the smallest tin of mackerel in tomato sauce that is cheaper and affordable. But chicken back is the marker of poverty. This is so in a country where chicken back is purchased wholesale in cases by well-to-do families to be fed to their dogs. And for families like the one I grew up in, chicken back could only be purchased in small portions, usually one pound (1lb.) for an entire family. So, at one point, the one pound (11b.) of chicken back was the daily dinner staple for seven (7) adults (me included) and one child. What this really meant was that the little meat, on the bony carcass of the chicken, that we could afford, was really mashed into gravy so eight (8) mouths could taste the little protein gravy over the rice or dumpling or bananas or breadfruit, or yam that formed the staple for our simple meal. And this was on a good day. On bad days there was no Chicken Back. Instead, there was something called So-So Food, i.e. food (usually ground provisions) prepared without any meat or protein. Really poor people from rural parishes like me also understood something called Fry-Up. Fry-Up was when you used home-made coconut oil (the homemade one you boiled and extracted from the coconut) to prepare a little meal accessory fried with salt, country pepper, and maybe a little onion or scallion if you were lucky. Fry-Up was made from ingredients that usually did not have to be purchased, so the onion or scallion was often optional.

That was a long time ago in my own life. But, while I have travelled very far in my personal journey to success, Chicken Back remains the protein of necessity, not of choice, for many of Jamaica's poorest citizens. Its updated companion, fish back, has joined the fray, especially after the year 2000. But when we speak of *Chicken Back Gravy* it sparks a response among many who have walked this road. *Chicken Back Gravy* is synonymous with hard life, desperation, marginalization and poverty. Yes, many of us have come from a very far place. And here we are.

So, this title—*Chicken Back Gravy and Such Delights*—one that I have used in many discussions—reflects the reality that I faced, as a young girl, teenager, teenaged mother and young adult. It speaks volumes about the reality of poverty and deprivation that was not of my own making—but into which I was born and from which I struggled to escape. What is comforting is that the reality of my early upbringing in Linstead, St. Catherine was masked by the similarities in the lives of most of my neighbours, and those children with whom I played. I didn't realise that we were so poor. I didn't understand the enormity of the chasm that I would have to breach. That clarity...harsh and painful...would begin to come later at high school—St. Jago High in Spanish Town, St. Catherine—where I was unceremoniously ripped from innocence and flung into understanding.

The little stories that form the basis of my *Chicken Back Gravy and Such Delights* story, along with the life lessons in this book are my gift of gratitude to those on whose backs I stand. And my contribution to my brothers and sisters—black people wherever you are, Africans in the diaspora wherever you are, Caribbean people wherever you are, Jamaicans wherever you are... and specially to those who remain locked in cages of poverty—wherever you are. But this work is also for those who, like myself, have broken free from the cages of poverty, but remain encased in the memories. We who remain transfixed by the portraits of black brothers and sisters whose daily and sometimes futile struggle for escape are stark reminders of how far we have to go on this journey called life in this place called Yaad. We must always remember who we are.

This first volume of *Chicken Back Gravy and Such Delights* is a piece of my heart that I am sharing with you. Reading this book will give you not just Life Lessons that I hope will benefit you, but also some brief insight into Who I Am and Why I Am this particular person.

I gift you these words with lots of Love and Endless Blessings.

Professor Donna P. Hope

LIFE LESSONS

Life Lesson #1
Know Yourself

"Who am I? The Girls Dem Sugar"
Beenie Man, *Who am I/Sim Simma*, 1997

One must always begin at the beginning. And so the first Life Lesson I learnt, and which I am sharing with you, was **to know yourself.** This means that you must engage with critical **Self-Knowledge** and come face to face with who you are, with all your positives and negatives clearly exposed. Self-knowledge, an understanding of who you are in the bigger scheme of things, does not usually come to children very quickly. Today, I give thanks for that because childhood innocence creates a protective shield that should allow young ones to grow and mature into the lives they have to lead without undergoing undue psychological and emotional stresses about their real situation of lack or otherwise. But, self-knowledge is a critical first step, and an important tool, on every journey towards success. Who am I?

StoryTime: A Little of MyStory

I am a Jamaican woman, raised in a single-mother headed household with my two brothers (one now deceased) in what was then a rural town, Linstead, St. Catherine. Linstead has developed so much today that it is scary when I visit—the development, the changes. Today all its streets, avenues and lanes are bursting at the seams with vendors and shops and people and cars. But back then when I grew up in the 1970s and early 1980s it was still a rural town. A rural feeder town for the many other rural communities and towns that surrounded it. Places like Bog Walk, Church Road, Knollis, Cotton Piece, Ewarton, Orangefield, Jericho, Burtons, Commodore, Princessfield, Buxton Town, Banbury, Heathfield, Wakesfield, Everybody came to Linstead—the center. And Linstead Market was the pride of place. When things were good, i.e. when there was a little money in the household. it was fantastic on a Saturday to go to Market with Mama. To sit on the handcart with the basket full of ground provisions, and the bunch of green banana and bag of grocery at the end of the shopping and be wheeled home to Gillette Street by "Pretty" or another one of the regular handcart guys. And Grandmarket Night (Christmas Eve) was the biggest event of our lives! All the excitement and fanfare and crowds of people from all over St. Catherine and St. Mary and Kingston and foreign who came to ring in the Christmas from as early as 8pm until 6am or later! Every child was freed from whatever curfew they had for that one night. We could explore everything and everywhere and prowl the streets for the entire night in our little groups. Things were good and I loved my life.

Mama was a serious woman and very strict about parenting. We had to attend school and church and keep out of trouble because this was what she expected. Miss Edith did not play. The Pentecostal Church on Gillette Street was the place where we learnt about hellfire and brimstone and the Ten Commandments and Golden Text at Sunday School and basically got a religious foundation. Rural Jamaican families like mine were very big on church, even if parents, like my mother, were not regulars. I still remember studying the Golden Text for next Sunday and then reciting it "The Golden Text is taken from "Insert Scripture Here".

School was also serious business. Mama trained us from early that "pickney muss go school" (children must attend school). From Mr. Kidd's Basic School on Gillette Street to Linstead All Age School (now Linstead Primary and Junior High) on East Avenue things were pretty great! We walked to school, had great friends and neighbours and a great deal of love. We had enough to eat, good clothes to wear and, even though we moved around a lot, we still lived in nice houses. As a young child, I thought we were living a great life. But we were really very poor.

The Beginning of Understanding

I really began to understand how poor we were when things started to fall apart in primary school. Our small family suffered blows when my brother's father fell ill and was no longer contributing regularly to the household income. And then when I left the safety of Linstead, the place where I was always a special, bright child, to attend high school in Spanish Town, St. Catherine — a much larger and more urban setting I became even more aware of who I was. Some of these stories will come in a more fulsome way in my personal Memoirs and in some of my other motivational books. But I can say that attending school with the demands of bus or train fare and lunch money daily, in a household with almost no disposable income and two children in high school is not a joke. My absentee father made intermittent contributions to my welfare. My mother did ad hoc domestic jobs. By that time I had a step-father who was an alcoholic and so his contribution was depleted by his bills at various bars. High school was just hard. I was hungry most days. This was in the days before book rentals became a reality, so I had no text books. My uniforms were frayed. My shoes were falling apart. High school is a painful blur…a period of too many lows and a few highs, punctuated by the great friends and peers with whom I journeyed…and with whom I maintain lifetime links. But what is important about this leg of my journey, is that by the time I dropped out of St. Jago High school at 15 as a pregnant teenager, I knew very clearly who I was. That was the end of my innocence and the beginning of my understanding. I began to recognize and understand, very clearly, the reality of who I was. I asked myself many questions. And I asked myself Who am I?

Who Am I?

For me, this was a very difficult and painful coming-of-age experience. But looking back it was necessary. This question of WHO AM I? is the most important one you will ever ask yourself. The answers are the most critical keys that will open your roadmap. You cannot carve a pathway to your success if you do not know WHO YOU ARE at each leg of your journey. Without this self-knowledge, you will face obstacles and be unaware of their presence until it is too late because you did not realise they would hamper YOU. At that time, my frank responses included the following:-

A black girlchild of rural poverty.

A black girlchild for whom *Chicken Back Gravy* was an exalted meal.

A black girlchild with a future potentially similar to my childhood, almost already cast in stone.

A black girlchild with very limited options.

A poor black young woman with my children's future almost already cast in stone and confined to a life of poverty.

One very bright (smart) black girlchild who had received a Government Scholarship to high school.

A young woman with big dreams, far more grandiose than her situation promised.

A young woman who was determined to craft a pathway to her own transformation in spite of and regardless of all the barriers in her way.

Who am I? This is a question that you must pose to yourself along every step of the way. Who am I? And you MUST answer it. Along each leg of your journey you are the same person at the core, but you are always being manifested differently. You are always growing, changing, rising. Wherever you find yourself in life—age, gender, nationality, country, education, employment status, relationship status etc.—always ask yourself "Who am I?" In one country, say Jamaica, you may be more working class/poor. In another, say the USA, you are the same person, but this time you may be more black or African. In another you may be more a woman bounded by strict gender codes. Or more a man, with promised opportunities just out of finger's reach. In some situations, like in the workplace or your family, you may be young. Or old. Or a mixture. You may be underqualified. Or overqualified. But you must always KNOW YOURSELF in the place and time in which you find yourself.

Self-knowledge is a critical key to your success. Based on your own understanding of who you are in that time and place, based on your critical self-knowledge you can craft your way towards your most successful self. Without this self-knowledge you cannot move. You will remain pinned in place. You will remain locked in the cages that have been prepared for you and your generations, long before you were even a thought. And if you do move, it will only be very incremental. So ask yourself now WHO AM I?

Look in the mirror at yourself. Be frank and truthful. And ANSWER.

Knowing who you are, coming to grips with this knowledge and accepting it is not always easy. Many times, it is a painful process. This is so, because no one truly wants to acknowledge the reality of their deprivation. No one wants to acknowledge the reality of their addiction. No one wants to acknowledge the reality of their marginalization. Of their lack of acceptance. Of their invisibility. Of their abandonment. Of their failure. Of having abandoned their dreams. Of having given up—maybe too easily, too early. No one. I cried many tears and wrote thousands of words over decades in my journals and closets of poetry. But, in all of this, a frank and pragmatic assessment using these tools helped me to have a clearer picture of myself. WHO AM I? Self-knowledge helped me to always accept myself as a full and complete person however I turned up at that time. And in accepting and understanding myself and my reality fully, I have long been very deliberate about the steps I take and the choices I make. Self-Knowledge helps me to practice Pragmatic Optimism; always with a clear understanding of Who I Am in this particular time and place. When you are able to do this with honesty and clarity, you are ready to take your journey towards true success.

So, as you work through the different and sometimes painful aspects of self-knowledge, get up every morning and look at yourself in the mirror. Alone.

Forgive yourself for your past. Forgive everyone else. Love yourself. Speak the words. "Who am I?" Who am I today? Answer yourself. And in knowing yourself, you can begin to fully BELIEVE IN YOURSELF. Believe that You can Do it. Believe that you will achieve your goals. Believe. Say the Words. "I can do it." Then get up out of your comfort zone and just do it. Do it every single day. And there you are.

Just a little over a decade later, I arrived at the University of the West Indies, Mona Campus. This place to which I had been journeying for some time has been the most fertile ground of my life. Bar none. My fantastic journey to that place, and onwards is being detailed in various other writings including my *Memoirs* and the second volume this *Chicken Back Gravy* series. But believe me, I walked many dark pathways, literally and figuratively, and sacrificed many treasures to arrive at the University, weighted down with the abundant responsibilities for my Son and my family and myself that I had acquired along the way. At that place, this place, the University of the West Indies at Mona under the guidance and with the support of some powerful men and women, I dug out of the earth some very important planks of my self-knowledge. Who am I? By that time, my responses to the question WHO AM I? had been transformed.

A young black woman of the rural working class. A young black woman for whom *Chicken Back Gravy* remained an option.

A young black woman with a present very different from my childhood and with the potential for an even greater future.

A young black woman with many options.

A struggling black young woman with my child's future transforming before my eyes.

One very smart (bright) black woman who was embarking on her University career to earn a Bachelors Degree.

A young black woman with big dreams, far more grandiose than her situation promised.

A young black woman who was determined to craft a pathway to her own transformation in spite of and regardless of all the barriers I her way.

I completed my Bachelors Degree with First Class Honours working against many odds. As I like to tell it, I almost starved to death a few times. This is not an exaggeration. But I succeeded by putting my shoulder to the wheel and with the full emotional and physical support of my mother and the emotional support of a few friends and key mentors along the way. And with the help of four (4) Students Loans over the four years of my degree programme (2 years part-time and 2 years full-time). My educational, professional and personal journey set the foundation for my life today. I am a possibility. I am always becoming. And I can win. Once you gain self-knowledge and the acceptance of all aspects of your reality then your confidence spurts upward. You begin to believe in the You that You are. And you begin to believe that you can do this thing that you set out to do. This is what I did and it worked. I stood in the mirror many times and asked that same question WHO AM I?

Today, these are my responses:-
A black woman from the middle classes.
A black woman for whom *Chicken Back Gravy* is a choice.
A black woman with a present filled with wonders and a great future.
A black woman with overflowing options and opportunities.
An independent black woman with an adult Son who continues to accomplish his goals.
One very smart (bright) black woman who is a tenured University Professor holding a PhD, MPhil. and a BA, an accomplished author, renowned speaker and motivator.
A black woman whose dreams continue to be fulfilled.
A black woman whose determination, confidence and hard work shattered many barriers and crafted a pathway to her own transformation.

You are the only person you will have to live with all your life. Remember this. So you must know yourself. SELF-KNOWLEDGE comes with your frank answers to the question WHO AM I? If you are not satisfied with your responses, then you must GET UP and TRANSFORM your life.

Life Lesson #2
Reading is a Great Gift.
And a Tool for Success

"Reading maketh a full man…and woman"

The second lesson I learnt very very early in life was that **reading is a great gift**. And a tool for Success. If you use it well, it becomes one of the "talents" that is bestowed upon you to enrich your life. If you maintain it, then it becomes a constantly evolving legacy. My life experiences confirmed this. Reading profusely, first out of curiosity, then for fun, and eventually also as a major part of my work-life and career, has been a major plank of my success.

StoryTime—My Life as a Reader

I did not "learn" to read in the traditional way at school. No. Reading was Mama's gift to me. She was an avid reader all her life with a great thirst for knowledge about other lives, other places and other people. Mama read constantly while I was in her womb. And then I watched her as a baby reading the Jamaican Star and Gleaner newspapers to the light of the Home Sweet Home kerosene lamp. I watched her as a toddler reading books, thick books, thin books, books with fantastic titles, books that made her serious, others that made her smile, and some that made her laugh out loud. And so I wanted to read those books because I realised that there was something special inside those pages. Yes, I wanted to read, and to know.

Living in the two room board house in Mr. Calloo's tenement yard on Montgomery Avenue in Linstead, we had no electricity. We had no television. We had battery-operated radios. But that was the way it was for almost everyone who lived around us. At nights we would light up the Home Sweet Home kerosene oil lamps inside and sit outside in the yard telling Anancy stories and Bredda Takuma stories and duppy (ghost) stories under the moonlit skies. And in all of this, my Mama would read and read and read and read and read. That was her main form of recreation after taking care of her household duties. That woman could read. I was always so intrigued by this thing. It was in my DNA. So, of course, as soon as I could make out words I was there reading right alongside Mama by the light of the Home Sweet Home kerosene lamp at nights. Most Jamaicans from rural backgrounds or poor families can relate to the warm, yellow, homely glow of this lamp. I began reading at two years old. Those little black squiggles on the newspaper's pages and in those books began to make sense. I have never stopped reading for pleasure. Never.

I began by reading the same Gleaner and Star newspapers

that Mama devoted her time to every day. And moved into reading the Bible, and books with strange titles… big books, small books. Romance novels and dramas and fiction and non-fiction. I read once-upon-a-time and they-lived-happily-ever-after fairytales from all over the world; with that knight in shining armour coming to save the day. I read Dr. Seuss and Enid Blyton's fanciful works that gave me ideas about difference and fabulous beings who all made life funny and very interesting. I read Don Quixote and Sancho Pancho. And then during my years at Linstead All Age School, I was given free rein to visit the library whenever I wanted by the time I was in Grade 5 (having skipped grade 4). I read everything in the Linstead School Library, which was my most favourite place at school. And then I read everything in the Children's Section at the Linstead Branch Library so they gave me special access to the Adult Section by the time I was 10 years old. Then, when I had read everything they had to offer at the Linstead Branch Library, they told me I had to transfer to the Parish Library in Spanish Town. That was a wonderful adventure—roaming those shelves in the Spanish Town Parish Library. I read and read. And then I met sci-fi and horror at 11 years old during my time at St. Jago…Isaac Asimov, Stephen King, Robin Cook, Jo Clayton, Frank Herbert and so many others. One of my teachers had a wonderful collection of Science Fiction and I read all of those as well. I read everything including the Penthouse and Playboy magazines that my friends furtively smuggled into classes. My mind was wide open.

I have never stopped reading for the love of it.

It is true that "reading maketh a full man" and woman, and boy and girl. Reading provided me with free passage into worlds from the past, ideas about the future and places which no one I knew had ever visited. Reading widened all my horizons beyond my limitations of gender, race, class and geography. I was born in a poor family and raised in situations that ranged from poor to very poor to poverty but my mind was rich with ideas about other ways that people lived here in Jamaica, and elsewhere in the world. We had no television, like so many of our neighbours, but my mind was filled with images of people from the past, present and future, and even some who were simply fanciful imaginations. Every single story, every single newspaper article, every single book gave me ideas about different ways to live life. I remember reading the story set in Holland about "A Leak in the Dike" as a very young child in Basic School. That fascinating lesson stuck with me for life. How a small child with a great understanding of their society, could literally save lives and property with a simple, selfless act — the placing of a finger in a hole in the Dike, the waterway. That finger served as a barrier to safeguard the Dike walls from giving in to the pressure from the water it held even while that child put himself at risk of death. She lived and her town was saved. Whether that story was true or not, fables and parables like those from all over the world taught me life's lessons and mantras that I still live by. I read every sign on the street, on the stores, on the billboards. I read everything. Everything I read taught me about the wonders of the world in which we live and opened my mind up to the possibilities that far outstripped my humble beginnings in Linstead. I learnt well about the power of words to inform ideas and to shape thoughts, which lead to action, and so contribute to positive transformation in the lives of individuals and larger groups.

My entire life is a testimony to this. Today my work is with words — teaching, researching, writing, mentoring, communicating — words are my tool and my salvation. Words kept me sane during the longest, darkest hours of my life and words have provided me with the happiest moments in my life. The written word is a real treasure that I carry through my life. I still spend more money on books than the average person. And I still believe that words can make a real difference. They made a difference in my life, first providing me with Hope and an understanding of my world. And also actively taking me from a life consigned by fate to the poverty of *Chicken Back Gravy* as the ideal meal, hopefully more than once per week, to whatever I want to eat, whenever I want it, moving my life from a stage of lack to one of abundance. The love of words and reading consistently made a difference in my life, moving me from under the bottom of the pile to holding my own in my career and other endeavours in

Jamaica and all over the world. Words and the love of words has been a critical part of my development and my success. I consider each and every piece of written work that I have published to date—my academic books, my newspaper and journal articles, my Facebook posts—all are crucial pieces of who I am that I share with the world.

Enrich Your Mind and Sharpen Its Capacity

Therefore, based on my own experiences and the value I have gained from reading, I am underscoring that point that "Reading maketh a full man, but moreso a successful man or woman". This is an important lesson from my life's journey. But I want to make it clear that this is not an overnight success. This making or re-making of yourself into a more successful version can take many years. It can take ten, fifteen, twenty or more years. Indeed, there is a little saying that: "It takes twenty years to become an overnight success". This is true in many instances. Reading will not make you successful overnight, but developing the habit of reading as a critical tool towards your success is something I must highlight. This is especially so in a world where reading has become seen as an antiquated activity. Many ask questions such as: Why read when it is all pre-packaged nicely in a video somewhere? Why read the book when the movie is there? Why NOT read the book to see the depth of expression that cannot be captured in the movie? Why not read the book to make your OWN interpretation of the writer's thoughts on paper? Your OWN interpretation which may differ greatly from the scriptwriter and/or the producer of the flick on silver screen? You would be surprised. Another response is usually "Reading takes too much time". I say that "People make time for the things and people that matter to them". So, if you want to transform your life then you have to learn how to do so. You have to open your mind and fill it with ideas that set you on this path. So, in order to enhance your mind you have to fill it with ideas. This means you must Read. Read everything. Read every label, every sign, every poster, as many newspaper articles as you can. Read blogs on the internet. Read motivational posts on social media. And read books in soft copy on smartphones, tablets, laptops or computers. Or in hardcopy (the ones I love the most) with the smell and feel of paper providing a tactile and aural backdrop to your mental enrichment. Just READ.

Reading exercises your mind and strengthens its capacity. Reading at least one page of something every day opens your mind to new horizons. Even if it is a single paragraph from an inspirational book. Reading every single day exercises your brain and provides you with clear information about life around you and life in other places. Reading helps you to prepare for different aspects of your life's journey. Indeed, you must always read ahead to prepare for different aspects of your life's journey, for example something as simple as getting directions to something a little more complex like preparing for a job or scholarship interview. Or other complex matters like a job change, a promotion or starting a business. Then there are more complex matters like dealing with significant life changes such as death, divorce, migration or depression. Somewhere in your group, community, country or in the rest of the world, someone has written something down about this matter. Find it and read it. And if you can't understand something clearly, read the meaning somewhere — on the Internet, in a Thesaurus or a Dictionary. Your mind is the most powerful tool you will ever have. Therefore, when you enrich and sharpen it with knowledge it will serve you with excellence.

An enriched and sharpened mind filled with a variety of knowledge will help you as it did me, to craft your roadmap out of your current situation. It will help you to face myriad situations with the calm assurances that you have read about this before. It will help you to prepare adequately for tough situations that must always come. You will KNOW that others have been here and survived so you will too. You will KNOW that there are rich possibilities behind this barrier. You will KNOW with great certainty as I did, that it is really true that "Behind every dark cloud there is a silver lining". I KNEW this and BELIEVED it, not just because people repeated it constantly, but because I read so many fiction and non-fiction stories that presented clear examples of the truth of this saying.

We are now living in the Knowledge Age. Reading is the most practical way to engage with and internalise knowledge about life and the world in which you live. Reading provides you with a portal into many different boardrooms, situations and activities that can positively impact your life's journey. And reading encourages you to balance your perspectives so you can live a life that is rich with possibility in today's world filled with diversity. Ignore those who rubbish the enrichment and sharpening of your mind. Ignore those who tell you they already have all the answers so you need not look any further. They are everywhere, claiming to be able to lead you to your true potential. Ignore those who try to tell you how to be who you are and who you want to be. For you to climb to new heights you must understand that you are in the depths. And you must also equip yourself with the knowledge and information about how to climb out of those depths so that you can achieve the success that you desire and deserve. Reading helps you to understand how to do it.

Life Lesson #3
You Can Do It,
You Can Always Do It

"Just do it"
Nike, 1988

The third Life Lesson I am sharing with you is also one I learnt very very early. This Life Lesson #3 is that **You Can Do It. You Can Always Do It.**

When we are very young children, we are all rich with the promise and possibility of our youth, and covered with the innocence of our years. This is so regardless of your circumstance of birth. Indeed, it is common practice in Jamaica to hear very poor parents expressing the desire or hope that their baby will become "the next Prime Minister" or "A Doctor" or "A Lawyer" or someone else of high status. There are similar hopes and desires in every Caribbean society and anywhere and everywhere that people of African descent find themselves. Many times, these hopes and desires are based on what is considered to be the career or profession that will guarantee that child (and hopefully his/her family) a pragmatic route out of poverty to success. Underlying this hope and desire is a clear expectation that such a transformation will also result in social and financial mobility. But children do not have these dreams. They are usually busy with their own happiness and dreams until life teaches them otherwise. Every young child is cast in this state and their innocence is a platform for happiness and big dreams. I was one such child. A child rich with promise and potential, a very gifted and very happy child. And I was taught very early the importance of my possibility and of my ability to Do It. To Always Do it.

StoryTime — Train Up a Child

Living in Linstead, St. Catherine in Jamaica, I first attended Mr. Kidd's Basic School on Gillette Street. The first time I stood in front of an audience to recite a poem I was just about a shade over two years old. They felt I could do it. Everyone did. I think it was graduation day or a concert at the school, or some other fanciful event. But I remember very clearly, after spending time learning the poem, that day I was preened and prodded by Mama and my teacher and some other ladies (other parents?). These nice ladies took me through the back door to be placed on what was then the BIG stage in front of the schoolroom, now turned into a packed audience of parents, teachers, friends — everyone.

For a child barely over two it looked like a HUGE audience and I remember looking down into those eyes, all staring up at me. Suddenly I realised that there was no one else on stage, no one but me. Mama and my teachers and all those nice ladies had retreated and left me alone with those EYES…all staring and getting bigger and rounder as if they were about to devour me. No one had told me about those hungry, hungry eyes. And so, of course I did what any sensible toddler would do under those circumstances — burst into tears! My rescue was swift, my tears dried, and nice ladies whispering soothing sounds "hush hush". And then my Mother and my teachers and those nice ladies did something that was a great gift that would serve me well. They put me right back on stage encouraging me to "do it", "do it". I did it. And, at the end of my recitation, I received resounding applause and hugs and kisses and wonderful rewards. But the greatest reward I learnt as a toddler not yet three years old was that I Can Do It. Always. You Can Always Do It at just a shade over two years old. If you fall, get up and try again. You can do it. That Lesson has stayed with me my entire life. You Can Do It. Just Believe.

Believe In YOU

For you to advance towards any goal, you must begin from a perspective of belief in yourself. You must convince yourself that YOU can do it, no matter what. You must believe that you can fumble, you can falter and you can even burst into tears, but you can still do it. Yes, it is true that you can retreat and take a little time out (not too much) to regain your strength. But you can do it. So you must get right back up on that stage of life and complete your journey. You must fulfil your potential. That was another very important lesson that I learnt very early that has been a foundation for all that I have achieved. You can do it. No matter what. Even after a million false starts. Once you set your mind to it, BELIEVE in yourself and get going, YOU can and WILL do it. And you will do it well. And when you really need them, angels will surround you and bear you up. Angels in the form of people like your mother, your father, your brother, your sister, your friends, your teachers, your mentors, and sometimes strangers along the way. You can and WILL do it.

Someone asked me "HOW" do you get to this point where you BELIEVE in YOU so much that nothing can shake your confidence? How do you achieve this so that you continue going, no matter what? The road to self-confidence can be difficult but it is necessary for your journey to success. Every single task that you approach must be backed by this confidence in your abilities. To be fully self-confident, to believe in YOU, you must first ensure that you prepare adequately. Again, Life Lesson #2 is important. Whatever task you move towards as a part of your ultimate goal, must be approached with critical knowledge about WHAT this task is. You must READ everything about this task. I studied my poem so that I would be able to deliver it. You will have to read about starting a company before approaching anyone to initiate this start-up. Before you approach the bank for seed funding, you must read everything about what the bank will need and ask for in order to qualify. Before you approach the scholarship application, read everything on the website and find out details from others who have been on that route. READ. ASK. Life Lesson #1 is also useful here. You must know WHO YOU ARE so that you approach the task with full self-knowledge. If you have a race to run, you cannot have a good chance of winning if you do not adequately prepare. Preparation includes daily training, proper diet and adequate rest. But it also includes the confidence that engenders a winning mindset so you can succeed. You must therefore know WHO YOU ARE, and what YOU will need to do in order to win. I knew WHO I was when I was on that stage. But I was not prepared for the HUNGRY eyes. No one had EVER told me about them. And no one had ever told me about the BUTTERFLIES in my stomach and the strange feelings that would overpower me. I had to learn that through experience. But I learnt well and recovered quickly. And I kept those lessons for LIFE. So you have what I call the **inside-out** aspect of self-confidence, which is always the most powerful. You KNOW that you are ready when you have pre-pared adequately and you feel that surge of confidence. You step to the examination room KNOWING that you got this. And then there is the **outside-in** aspect of self-confidence that comes from the people who know how you are and who you are and who give you their props and support. These people are your support system, your cheering squad, your motivators. Some are people with whom you have worked or interacted and who have confidence in your abilities. Do not confuse them with fans and fake friends who come and go like the wind. But once they are genuine and frank, these outside-in people will give you a glimpse of yourself from the outside that can encourage you to higher levels of self-confidence, and generate higher levels of belief in your abilities. What is also important in this powerful mantra of doing and succeeding at doing it? You should know as much as you can about whatever it is you plan to do, be or achieve. About yourself, about the place in which you find yourself. About the journey ahead, and what came before.

I have stood on many, many stages in Jamaica, the Caribbean, the USA, Europe and elsewhere in the world. And I have hosted and chaired so many events that they all blur into each other. But it all started on a tiny stage not so long ago in the distant past. They held my hand, pushed me back on stage, but I had to overcome my fears and to believe in myself and the wisdom of those wiser than me. Once you begin to Believe in yourself and to gain that confidence, then you will have to put it into practice. When you are faced with frightening situations, when eyes and circumstances seem ready to devour you…remember, You can Do It. You can Always Do it. And you are entitled to falter, to fall, to fail and to try again. But you must always get up and DO IT regardless of your situation.

Life Lesson #4
Poverty is Not a Nice Thing

"It's a competitive world for low budget people, spending the dime while earning the nickel"
Untold Stories, Buju Banton, 1995

The fourth lesson I learnt very early in life was that **Poverty is not a nice thing.** "Poverty is not a nice thing" is a pretty simple statement. It sounds a bit cliché but I use it very often and without apology. There are many apologists and do-gooders who will say otherwise. There are those who encourage the poor to seek pies in the sky, and tell you about the great things that will come in the afterlife. But, as someone who has come from the depths of poverty, as one of the original *Chicken Back Gravy* massive, one who has had to live with little to no food at times, one good suit of clothing at times, sometimes not even a decent pair of shoes, let me underline this — **Poverty is an unnatural condition of the human existence.** The world in which we live has all things in abundance so that all humankind can live without want and with dignity and love, even while some have too much and others have too little. And so, the natural inclination of human beings is to move towards the good life, that is, a life that is better than that which you find yourself encaged in.

If you have faced deep poverty, been poor or found yourself in a situation of lack, you will find that some persons romanticize poverty. Oh, they chirp, the simplicity of your existence! The purity! I wish I could escape this prison of materialism and live simply. The usual garbage from those who have an *option* to choose to live in rustic, earthy simplicity today and return to their lives rich with every comfort that money can buy in a heartbeat. I particularly love to hear this from white foreigners whose legacies of imperialism mean that even while living at the barest minimum in their homeland, they can afford to visit countries like Jamaica for a vacation in "Paradise". How exotic. These are the folks who will tell you how lucky you are to be living in a little wooden shack on the side of a river… or in a community with no amenities…no proper roads, electricity or garbage collection networks. Your Paradise is a place where every single meal is a crisis. Oh yes, you are told that you and your family are blessed. What they are always careful to never speak about is how this "Paradise" which is your existence and your one and only harsh reality, is but a momentary break, a temporary time away from their "real" lives. It is only ONE of the multiple realities that they can afford to CHOOSE to have at any point in time. I have always been terrified of these people. These are the ones who desperately need you to remain who you are and where you are so that you can provide a mirror for them to see themselves in all their greatness.

There are also the meaningless platitudes from those others whose religious comforts are often like barbs in the souls of those who face the brunt of poverty every single day. The usual "something something" to the notion that you are so blessed in poverty on earth that you will go to heaven. Yes, you are **guaranteed** a space in heaven because "it is easier for a camel to go through the eye **of a needle than for a rich man to enter the Kingdom of Heaven"**. These meaningless platitudes are small comfort when you cannot even afford a needle. "Money is the root of all evil" they chirp! (The actual verse says "For **the love of** money is the root of all evil").

Story Time — The Means Test

I came to an understanding of myself as an individual in Mr. Calloo's tenement yard on Montgomery Avenue in Linstead, St. Catherine, Jamaica. Aside from a tiny handful, most of our neighbours were living similar lives, and so it took me a very long time to realise we were poor. Really poor. My environs of Montgomery Avenue, Gillette Street, Coghill Town, Mr. Kidd's Basic School and the Linstead Pentecostal Tabernacle all provided safe haven. We played in our yard and on Montgomery Avenue, and then on Gillette Street and elsewhere, without a care in the *world. The fact that Mama kept moving house, first from Montgomery Avenue to a bigger and nicer place on Gillette Street at Mr. Fuller's house, and then all around Linstead, did not strike me as an issue….at first. And when I moved to big school at Linstead All Age School on East Avenue, all the teachers welcomed me, as a bright child, with open arms. By the time I left Linstead All Age School for St. Jago High School in Spanish Town my family's situation had worsened. I was the prodigy at Linstead All Age School, but even a Government Scholarship with its grand stipend of J$40.00 per school year could not keep me from the daily struggle to find bus fare and lunch money every day. Especially since J$35.00 of that $40.00 had to be used to pay what was then called the Caution Fee, due each school year at St. Jago. I remember in particular that it was close to that time when Mama applied for what was then called Poor Relief and the lady came to do the residency aspect of the Means Test. I had no idea what that was at the time. These terms and their understanding came to me decades later. But what I remember very clearly is how Mama set her face like it was in concrete when she put on her clothes to go down to the Poor Relief Office to apply. And how agitated she was when she came home and told us that the lady from the office would have to come and make a visit. And then how her face looked when the lady arrived. It was the first time I saw my mother with that look. She was ashamed, Mama was so embarrassed. Her discomfort grew as she watched the lady walk through the two rooms in which we lived and count the number of beds, the number of rooms,* *how many of us lived there. The lady went outside to our kitchen and counted the plates and forks and knives and pots. She went to our bathroom and our toilet. That lady noted everything on the document on her notepad. And I still remember the look on that lady's face. She could not hold a neutral face. No. There was a kind of controlled pity and horror all rolled into one running across her face. Hadn't she ever seen poor people before I wondered? At the end of that ordeal, my mother refused to return to the Poor Relief office to finalise the paperwork so we could start receiving the small benefit. I was about ten years old but I started to understand our Chicken Back Gravy reality very clearly. And so, I began to lay down in my head the roads I would not walk. My Rules for Life.*

Rules for Life

Poverty is a harsh reality that many like me have faced and many continue to face. It was not a personal choice. I did not take a vow of poverty and renounce worldly goods as a part of some religious or personal journey. I was never allowed to choose whether or not I wanted *Chicken Back Gravy* as my only most ideal option. Poverty is not a nice thing when you cannot afford your basic necessities. It is not a nice thing when every meal is a crisis. Every single meal an insurmountable task that your family must plan and plot and scheme to achieve every single day. And so, as soon as I began to understand my *Chicken Back Gravy* reality, I renounced that choice made for me before I was born by others with more power in my own society and others from elsewhere. I accepted the reality of my situation. This is who I am now. But this is not who I will remain. This is where I am now. But this is not where I will remain. In doing so I took back my power.

This laying down of rules for life is a critical step in challenging poverty. Indeed it is a critical step in challenging any situation that locks you in a cage. To change your situation, to transform your life, you must first acknowledge your reality. To challenge any negative situation, you must first name it. Call it for what it is. Then you must confront it for what it is. And then you must renounce it. Reject it. And then you must begin to work against it with all your might. The change is always within you. But first you must claim this change as your own. You must acknowledge it as your birthright. And then you must breathe life into it. Why? Why not? Because once you claim this, then you can begin to lay down the rules that will govern your life. These include rules about the roads you will and will not walk (or will try to or try not to) as well as rules about the things you will and will not do (or will try to or try not to).

I think that everyone who goes along life's journey has these kinds of rules for the road that they develop along the way. You know the kind of thing that comes upon you as you go along? I will never allow my children to face this kind of poverty. I will ensure that I do not face this kind of embarrassment. I will do whatever it takes to provide for my family. I will have a future filled with far more delights than my present. Sometimes these rules are easy to lay down but very hard to live up to. This is the sad part of many realities. We make these rules. We swear by them. But when the time comes to take the decisive steps, we falter, we are afraid. We are AFRAID. I tackle this issue of FEAR in Life Lesson #6 and give you some tips from my own experiences on how to challenge this FEAR and beat it back in order to move on. What I can say here is that we see the challenges, we swear we will change it, but then we are afraid. We are timid. Poor people do not have the luxury of giving in to fear. You must BE BRAVE. Take up your bed and WALK. RUN WID IT.

My family lived in twelve (12) different rented places in Linstead by the time I was 20 years old and began working to be able to take over the reins of our household fully. By that time we had been evicted, cotched with relatives, and lived in some of the most impoverished sections of Linstead. We had suffered significant fallout in the already financially strained lifestyle that I had come to know as a child. My blood still runs cold when I remember some of those moments, the stress, the fear, that knot in your stomach…how worried I was about moving—AGAIN. Yes, I remember how I watched life beat my mother and my family down and grind us deep into the dirt and there I was, too young to be able to do anything about it. Yet, even though we had never lived in our own home, home ownership was an elusive dream that my mother pursued. At one point, Mama wanted a "government house"; and at another she wanted a piece of land to build something on. Mama didn't want to "live on capture land" because she didn't want to face eviction sometime in the distant future. But, as a woman with limited education, no financial resources and no real source of income this remained a dream that eluded my mother her entire life. I watched the entire story unfold. And, so, this elusive dream of home ownership was another goal that I set as a part of my rules that I developed along the way. More than just that, I wanted to be a landlord. Today I AM. Poverty and hard life can be great motivators. And so, you must use WHATEVER situation you find yourself in to motivate you to create RULES that will direct your path. And you must STICK to your PATH and live up to your RULES.

There are these lessons I am sharing with you about poverty and about transformation. These can be applied not just by the *Chicken Back Gravy* massive, but to anyone who is seeking to transform his or her life from a negative situation. Listen. When you decide to change your situation, for example to move from the depths of poverty to another level, brace yourself. If you want to move from one stage of life to another more improved or higher standard, prepare adequately. There are no benefactors. If help does come it will have strings attached. Always. You will have to pay for it. In cash or kind. In blood or sweat or tears—or some mixture of these. Sometimes you will not be willing to pay the price. Sometimes you will. Sometimes you will have to soldier on. Brace yourself. You will be your best friend and your main support. Sometimes you will have to motivate yourself by yourself, from within. And, if you are a poor, black young woman from the working classes, or a poor black young man from the inner-cities or rural poverty, you will have to fight many, many battles. Brace yourself and put on your armour and prepare for lots of hard work up ahead. I knew that I would have to brace myself for some serious hard work. And so I did. You can too.

Life Lesson #5
Poor People Have to Work Hard, Harder, Hardest. And Smartest

Labor Omnia Vincit.

I am a living testimony to this **Life Lesson #5** that **Poor people have to work Hard, Harder, Hardest. And Smartest.** What you must understand, however, is that there is nothing personal in this. It isn't that no one likes you. There is no personal vendetta against you. This is just the way that most of our social systems are structured all over the world. Poor people, those most deprived, will not be given a free pass. They will not be given a jump in the line. They will have to work harder than everyone else. And even when you have won the race, you will have to win it twice, maybe three times more. You will have to PROVE that you have earned it almost every single time. Again, this is nothing personal but rather a component of how your society is arranged. This is a lesson that you must learn even before you begin the race.

The reality is that poor people, poverty-stricken people, however they are manifested in whichever society they find themselves, usually get little more than the scraps that are thrown from the tables of those more fortunate because charity is just that. Charity. It is not about elevating everyone out of their situation. No. Poor people are important. They keep the social balance intact. Every society needs its poor, its marginalized, its deprived, and its always-available bodies so that the balance of power can be maintained. There can be no rich people if there are no poor people. What would be the basis for comparison? This is the reality. Once you recognise this, you will recognise how hard your journey will be. You will recognize that you will have to give up more to get less. And you will have to give up something, whatever that is, to get ahead. This is what we refer to as Opportunity Cost. Something always has to be given up in order for something else to be gained. This is a bit like the bird in the hand and those two in the bush story. What no one ever explains very clearly is that, if you want those two birds in the bush, you will have to let go of the one in your hand. The one in your hand that you let go is your Opportunity Cost. You have to give up to get more. And you can neither be too angry or too bitter about this. Indulging in anger and bitterness about how hard you have to work and how much you have to pay for your small movement will hamper and distract you. So you cannot linger there long. And then, if you are able to accept this reality you will be able to move forward.

When you decide to climb out of poverty, to dig yourself out of a situation of lack or to transform your reality, you will have to work. Hard. Let me repeat. You will have to Work. Hard. You will live the terms Opportunity Cost and Delayed Gratification. Delayed Gratification is just that — delaying or putting off having things that you like or like to do or things that you love or love to do and the pleasure you get from indulging in them. You have to put off having or doing these things and feeling pleasure from this activity, i.e. you delay your access to them, so that you can achieve this bigger or more important thing. And, you will also have to practice self-discipline. If you apply yourself in this way, you will discover that there is really no such thing as a free lunch. If you get it free, i.e. you pay nothing directly for it, not even a little labour, then someone else is paying for it in cash or in kind. Now, I am not suggesting that there aren't those fortunate few who break through easily and quickly. These lucky persons exist in every society. In Jamaica we have our dancehall artistes and our superstar sportsmen and women. And those few who also hit it big in our National Lottery game, the Lotto. Other countries have their Lottery winners, their music mega-stars, their millionaire sportsmen and women, their popular film and TV stars. Chances are, you may not be so lucky. While you wait on chance to strike like the proverbial lightning, continue to work towards your personal goals and dreams. Work.

StoryTime — A Slice of Working Hard

My first two years at UWI were completed part-time while holding down a full time job at what was then Cable and Wireless, (formerly JTC then TOJ) which eventually morphed into LIME and then subsumed into FLOW. That company was pretty decent with its educational opportunities. I got a single, full-day release on a Wednesday, during the first two years that I studied part-time to earn my Bachelors Degree. To make sure that I covered my desk, I would work late in the office on the Tuesday evening, sometimes until after 11pm. Then I would leave Kingston by public transportation to get to Linstead, sleep for a few hours and then wake early to leave Linstead by 5.30am to go to UWI all day on the Wednesday. At 8.00pm every Wednesday, I would leave my classes or the library at the UWI and go to my office at Parkington Plaza and stay there until 10.30 or 11pm. Then I would make my way home to Linstead by public transportation. I could not afford to be paralyzed by fear. One cannot be afraid of gunmen and criminals and thieves when there are greater things in life to fear like poverty and deprivation and the huge levels of disrespect that come with this subject position. I KNEW who I was. And so I needed to cover my desk because I had a class on the Mona Campus at 8.00am on a Thursday and would be "stealing time" to come in to work late on a Thursday closer to 10am—even though work started at 8.00am. So, my desk had to be cleared every Wednesday night to make sure that my boss was not out of sorts. I never flinched. Not once. I never complained. Not once. Every time I hear someone complain about how hard their life is, I remember those days when I would make the lonely trek, walking at nights from Half Way Tree to Parkington Plaza to work until after 10pm and then make the lonely trek back up from Parkington Plaza to Half Way Tree to go around to Eastwood Park Road to get on a bus going to Spanish Town. And then reach Spanish Town and pray to see something, anything going to Linstead, since the minibuses and taxis usually stopped working by 10pm or a little after. This was before the advent of toll roads, and before the setting up of the UWI school buses, and before the overflowing numbers of route taxis on every route, and before all those nice additions to the public transportation system in Kingston and its environs. That public transportation system was the one my friends and I called "The Middle Passage" in tribute to its harsh, packed, smelly and overall chaotic situation. I remember it all very clearly—the smells, the sounds, the camaraderie, the pushing and the shoving. But when you are poor you must pay the price for your movement. The price is usually a composite of sweat, tears and blood.

Sweat, Tears and Blood

Sweat is the usual (and easiest) price you will ever pay for any of your achievements, however small or intangible. Poor people have a lot of sweat that they can translate into both tangible and intangible achievements. The challenge is that the conditions of modern life throw up all kinds of distractions that pretend to lead you towards achievements. But the truth is that all achievements come with real sweat and if you are a member of the *Chicken Back Gravy* massive all of your achievements will require sweat. If your only currency is your labour, your sweat, then this means hard work. Long hours. Working while others are sleeping. Labor Omnia Vincit — the motto of my primary and high schools. Labour Conquers All. Today there are many who tell you about how they are "living their best lives" simply because they say so and can too. But there is still work to do before this will lead to any real achievement. There may be feel-good moments and lots of love and likes on social media. But then you will have to invest real time in the real world to study and to sit the damn exam in order to pass it. You could parrot all the tried and tested mantras about "winning" but you will have to find the resources to pay for that degree — Students Loan, Scholarship, Grant, part-time job, whatever? And you will have to put time and energy into the coursework and exams to get the piece of paper. If you plan to start a company you will have to find the start-up capital (micro-financing funds, collateral loan, or personal loan) and you will have to invest your time, and your labour for free in order to nurture it from its baby stage, until it can actually launch and begin to return tangible rewards. Along the way you might lose it all since 50% of all small business fail in the first year. Yes, you will have to invest a great deal of sweat. And time. Just sitting and saying it, and expecting it to happen because you are poor and so you "deserve it" will not translate into anything tangible. Passing around memes on social media about "winning" and "living my best life now" doesn't mean anything in the real world if your parents did not have the resources to give you a head start. Know your damn self. Get up and go look it.

So, you must sweat the hardest NOW when your youthful (or not-so-youthful) body can deal with the stresses and pressures. I remember visiting my medical doctor in my early 20s because of recurring chest pains. Tests showed nothing. He asked me what I was doing and I told him of my hectic schedule. Leave home before 6am to catch the train or bus. Work until 4.30 or 5pm. Evening classes until 8.30pm 4 nights per week to reach home after 11pm (wicked public transportation system) Repeat on Fridays but go for after-work jam or movies until 11pm. Work all day Saturday, then rest and go out. Work half day Sunday then rest and prepare for the rest of the week. My Doctor was concerned that I was putting my body under too much pressure. I told him my story and explained that nothing would get in the way of my dreams. Nothing. He prescribed multi-vitamins for me. I have been taking multivitamins as a part of my life's routine for more than two decades. Poor people cannot sit back and expect they will get a single job or business somewhere that will make them rich forever. That is a pipe dream. I constantly encourage young people, and those not so young, to take up a second, part-time job so they can achieve personal goals. What better time than when you are young and have energy and time on your side? Working an extra eight hours per week—maybe in a weekend job on a Saturday or Sunday, or in an after-work job for two extra hours four days a week can provide you with the extra income to cover some goal. Time is what you have in abundance. And time is the substance of your dreams. Time is the currency of your life. Poor people have time in abundance. Manipulate it. Strategize when, how and why you will sweat. Make your sweat count.

Tears are the second easiest price you will have to pay. Sometimes the sweat and tears are so mixed up you have no idea which is which. You will cry for the battles you will lose along the way. You will feel despair after having worked long and hard to achieve something—a scholarship, a job, a promotion, a new car, a house—to have it taken out of your grasp. You will cry because you worked long and hard but you just cannot pull enough together to fulfil that promise to your child. Or your Mother. Or your spouse. There will be many slips between the cup and the lip. You will bawl. Heartwrenching, gut-tearing wails. But you will not give up. I have bawled. And screamed. But I have never given up. Salt water is an excellent therapeutic and healing liquid which will serve you well along your journey.

Of course, this discussion about tears does not mean or suggest that you will or are to become a crybaby. I say this because many persons, especially women, use tears as a form of emotional blackmail, even in professional, work situations. They weep or cry strategically to tug at the heartstrings of potential benefactors, supervisors and others. Many times, these can backfire and you can be seen as weak, or manipulative, or both.

Blood is the ultimate price you will have to pay along your journey. Hopefully, this will only be in a few instances. In the first instance, I use the term "blood" to stand in for those friends and family who will leave you along the way. Some will leave because of death. This is the most painful instance of all. Others will leave because they are unable to go with you to the next level. This will happen with your friends if you aim for higher and higher levels, and do achieve them. In the second instance, I use the term "blood" to stand in for when you will be called upon to suspend your standards or beliefs in order to cross over. This is where you will have to decide if your integrity, loyalty or other personal standard is worth the upward move. Many times, black women (and men) are implicitly (and sometimes explicitly) asked to engage in a transactional relationship that promises financial and professional rewards. The choice is up to you. How will you feel if you accept what I call a vertical promotion? That is, one based on the exchange of sexual favours with someone who is your superior or your immediate boss in an entity in which you work? How will you respond if or when asked to compromise your integrity and engage in a shady or outright illegal activity with your career or some personal advancement on the line? What will happen if you are found out? And if you are not? Everyone has different standards. You will have to decide what strikes at the core of your being and what you find unimportant enough to give up in exchange for a social, financial or professional reward. In all these foregoing instances, you will leave a part of you behind, whether by choice, or because it is a part of the journey of life and social mobility.

Hard work does not end with the first leg of your journey. If you plan to soar higher, then plan to work harder. Plan to sweat, cry and bleed more. I have worked four jobs, sometimes three jobs, here in Jamaica. All while studying and managing my responsibilities for my son and family. If you come from a poor family, why would you expect that a single job, a regular job, will give you enough resources to achieve your goals and dreams? That is the damn foolishness that is sold to poor people. "They should pay you more". The reality of our capitalist system is that no one is ever paid what they are worth. If you wish to exploit your skills and earn more, then open your own business and become an entrepreneur.

If you lack the capital and other resources to start a real business, as most poor individuals do, then you will have to work for someone else. If you are in a job (or holding down several) your job is not to count the cows. Don't worry about what your boss is getting and how you are being exploited. That is mere distraction. What you have to offer is your labour so maximise it. You will achieve your personal goals much faster if you have the resources to put behind them. And you will achieve these resources if you put in more time.

The other side to this working hard is in recognizing that you will face obstacles. There is no massive cheering squad complete with marching band and pom poms waiting on you, a child of poverty, to present yourself. You will have one or two key persons, usually your Mother and maybe a very good friend in your corner. And a few angels will turn up to greet you at each doorstep. But the reality is, once you breach those doors, you have arrived inside. And so no one really cares about where you came from. You are now HERE. And if you sing too much about how poor you are... boo hoo...you will not be taken seriously. Once you enter the race to success, you cannot use your humble beginnings as a crutch to show how broken and needy you are, or as a beating stick to bludgeon those more fortunate into giving you access. No. Even while you may be struggling to make ends meet along the way to your success, you cannot use this as a club to beat resources out of those with whom you interact. Those who control resources such as jobs and promotions are not handing them out like charity. There are other places where you go for charity. Here, you will have to work for and merit these resources. Where big money is concerned, remember that those with a lot of it, aka rich people, are always very wary about those who come from the base of society. Rich people remain rich because they do not give away their wealth. Don't be fooled. No one with wealth is looking to "help" you up. Brace yourself and put your labour to work for you.

The "Work Smart, Not Hard" mantra has merit when you apply it carefully. Sometimes working smart translates into working hard. How else will you move the mountain standing in your way? I remember working so hard that I fainted from sheer fatigue and had to be sent on sick leave from work to get bed rest because my body was totally drained. I still have that tendency but have learnt to recognize my body's warning signals. But back then during the hardest part of my journey, I could not slow down. I could not give up. Giving up was never an option.

Life Lesson #6
Never Ever Give Up.

Sea-bottom people nuh fraid ah shark.
Donna P. Hope

The sixth Life Lesson that I must share with you is to **Never Ever Give Up.** This means that you must also Be Brave. Throughout my entire life I have learnt a great deal about holding fast and never giving up. This is also directly related to what I learnt about never giving in to FEAR.

Giving Up Is Never An Option

As a young woman in her twenties, struggling against so many odds, and being battered and bruised by the storm of life, there were two things that I kept close to me both at work and at home. On the left side of my bed (or the right, depending on where the wall was) I pasted two photocopied images. One was a photograph of a frog, his arms (or front legs?) wrapped tightly around the neck of a stork. The frog is partially down the throat of this stork, but he is NOT GIVING

UP. The stork will either strangle or release him. Right? I still wonder about how that stalemate turned out. Maybe they are lost somewhere in infinity with the frog tightly gripping the throat of that stork forever. Who knows?

The other image was a print of a little saying that had been given to me by a friend:

"Every morning in Africa, a gazelle wakes up. It knows it must run faster than the fastest lion or it will be killed. Every morning a lion wakes up. It knows it must outrun the slowest gazelle or it will starve to death. It doesn't matter whether you are a lion or a gazelle: when the sun comes up, you'd better be running."

For many, many years, I would wake up and read that saying and look at the frog hanging on for dear life to the throat of the stork. And I would get up, give thanks for life and health, and keep running.

I also had these same images posted on the drywall directly over my typewriter at work for many many years. I kept my eyes on it when I was working. Or when I was frustrated, fatigued or just plain tired. Believe me when I say that they both gave me a great deal of motivation to keep going. I never knew who drew that Frog vs. Stork and, at the time I used it, the Gazelle and Lion fable typed and printed on paper had no author.

Then, there was (and still is) Psalm 23. "The Lord is

my Shepherd, I SHALL NOT WANT". That Psalm is still a mantra in my head. I recite it every time I am about to do something difficult, something that will take my resources. Sometimes I recite it using slightly amended words "The Lord IS my Shepherd, I HAVE NEVER WANTED". Listen to me. You have never really been in WANT. You have never starved to death, have you? The *Chicken Back Gravy* may have been poor people food, but you did not starve. You may have been hungry sometimes, but did you actually lose your life? No.

What I want you to understand from the story above is that your journey from *Chicken Back Gravy* (?) or on from wherever you are in your journey, to your transformation and success, must also be backed by appropriate motivational props and encouraging pieces. Because I started my journey at a time when the job of motivational speaker, life coach and such delights was not yet a big reality, I had to cut and paste, and make up my motivational package. There were no Jamaican motivational speakers and life coach gurus and people, barely wet behind the ears, telling you they will show you how to aspire and soar. As a child, and young adult, I had no television at home because we could not afford one. So I learnt that one must motivate from both within and without. You must feed your mind with the type of information that will boost your flagging spirits and failing body, and you must place appropriate pieces of motivational paraphernalia close by. Much later in life, when I had long passed over the harshest part of my journey, I began reading a few books, all from the USA, which gave some useful suggestions. Yet, I have always believed that there should be a growing cadre of Jamaican and Caribbean writers, who give real-life suggestions based on our own reality for people of colour in the African/Caribbean/Jamaican diaspora. Regardless of the lack or otherwise, I found my motivational props and used them to spur me along. You MUST find yours. I hope that these frank musings, along my pathway from *Chicken Back Gravy* to various Delights provides you with even a small part of that necessary foundation.

Because I never gave up, I had to be brave. Bravery in the face of fear is also a great asset along your journey.

Be Brave

A man told me recently that I am too brave for a woman. Brave? Of course, I couldn't understand his point as I have been Brave for so long that it is second nature. He said "You act as if you fear nothing, as if nothing can harm you". He clearly did not understand. I learnt a long time ago, along my journey, that there is really nothing to fear but fear itself.

Life's journey for everyone is about holding fast and overcoming obstacles against many different odds. For a child of real poverty, for someone who comes from a very poor background, who is seeking to transform his or her life against insurmountable odds, fear is a constant companion. Many of us are afraid of who we may become. We are afraid of upsetting the apple cart. We are afraid that THEY will say WE are not "humble"—even when this so-called humility is more of a self-effacing, servile posture that I had to rubbish from very very early. We are afraid that THEY will think WE are too aggressive—and this is especially so for women who are held fast in the gender structures that police inappropriate behaviour. In short, we are afraid of actually becoming all that we dreamed possible. We are afraid of shining too brightly. Because of this fear that carries so many different strands to it, many of us are not BRAVE. We are timid. We are afraid. Even with the best of intentions, even after we spent our early years looking at the situation of lack in our lives and dreaming about how we would change it. How we would be able to afford to eat something more than *Chicken Back Gravy*. How we would buy Mama a nice house. How we would send our children to the best schools. How we would buy a nice car. How we would move to live in a better neighbourhood. How we would travel abroad just for fun. How we would go on vacations. Yes. Say it with me. **"How we,—how I—would never allow this very bad thing to happen to us again"**. And certainly it would never happen to our children, not over our dead bodies. We made all these wonderful dream-statements, some sounding like rules for our lives, as we say in Jamaica "big and serious" rules that would never be breached. But, when the time comes, and we are faced with a life-changing decision, we are afraid. And so we do not act on them. We are not Brave.

During my years of transformation, I could not afford to be paralyzed by Fear because I was already far more terrified of Poverty. That terror made me BRAVE. Bravery did not and does not mean the absence of FEAR. This is something that I want to reinforce. You must reinforce it for yourself. I hope that man who said I was fearless, but really meant BRAVE, will read this book and understand. BRAVERY does not mean that you are not held deep in the grip of the most paralyzing **FEAR.** Of course not. What it means is that you choose to do something even though you are terrified. You choose to move onward and upward in spite of and regardless of the fear that grips your limbs. Even though every cell in your body is telling you: "NO. NO. Let us stay right here in our comfort zone". And even when everyone around you is going in another direction, or not going at all you bravely move towards YOUR goals. Yes, I was AFRAID, and I was also aware of the depths from which I would have to climb. At no time was I ever unclear about this. If I wanted to change my present and my future and assure my children a better past, present and future, then I would have to battle this overpowering FEAR. I would have to be BRAVE. In Jamaica we say "Nuh Watch Nuh Face". There have been several times during my journey when FEAR paralyzed me to the point where I could get no sleep for weeks, and when I did I had perpetual dreams of falling down deep dark depths, waking up from this nightmare with a terrible sinking feeling in my stomach. Here is one such instance.

StoryTime — Bravery Against the Odds

I am a Confidential Secretary to a Head of Department at what was then Cable & Wireless (formerly JTC and TOJ; then LIME and eventually bought out by FLOW). We were based at Parkington Plaza in Kingston. It was a good job which paid my bills, took care of my Son, my adopted Sister, Mama and me. It had full benefits, health card, pension, paid vacation leave etc. I was the only breadwinner for my family of four. By this time, I had completed two years part-time at UWI. Now, my BA in Mass Communication had to be completed full-time because of the amount of time necessary for our courses, especially our Specialization which had two four-hour classes each week. I had to go in full-time.

I applied for a staff scholarship from Cable & Wireless. This scholarship would fully fund the rest of my degree, and cover all my costs. At the end of my program I would be bonded to work with Cable & Wireless for the same period. I would also have to return to work during summer and Christmas breaks. I signed up the Scholarship Application form and submitted it to my HOD. The document was completed by him and sent by him under Confidential cover to our Training School on Camp Road where these matters were decided. Two days later I received a call from one of my friends inside the Training School. She was livid. She wanted to know what I had done to this man, because his poor evaluation of me meant that I would not get the scholarship. By the time the news came back to my Department I was well aware of it.

I remember going to UWI that July to register for my courses. Back then we had to physically register for our courses. CARIMAC's registration desk was based in the Old Library. I went by faith because up to that moment I did not know how I would find the resources to go to school full-time and survive. Advancing to the CARIMAC registration desk, I took up the form, and filled in the list of full-time courses. I remember clearly looking at the form and being unable to tick Full-Time. Because I could not. I completed everything on the form but my hand was paralyzed over that one tiny section. Full-Time vs. Part-Time. How would WE survive? To come in full-time back then meant I would have no job and so I would have no means of support for my family who depended solely on me. And I would not be able to take care of myself. There were no part-time telemarketing jobs that you could craft your schedule around. No nothing. A CARIMAC Academic Advisor looked at me and recognized my hesitation. "I cannot come in full-time, I have to work". He responded "Donna, you have to decide now". Standing there in my blue Cable and Wireless uniform, I ticked the section marked Full-Time. Every drop of blood ran out of my body. I knew that I had just taken a huge leap of faith into something unknown.

I had just stepped off a cliff with no parachute and no knowledge of what lay below. For two weeks I did not sleep and I barely ate. I had constant nightmares about falling. Constant. One morning I woke up. Tired. But I had weighed all my odds and made my decision. It was time. That day, I went to work, and applied for my two weeks' vacation leave. Upon receipt of the final approval for my vacation leave from the Human Resources Department a few days later, I tendered my one month's resignation from Cable and Wireless.

Two weeks later, I was unemployed. I cashed in my pension and withdrew all my savings from the C&W Credit Union. I had already applied to the Students Loan Bureau to cover my tuition. But I did not know how I would make it for the two years full-time. How WE would make it. I was terrified. But I was BRAVE.

My full-time journey on the UWI, Mona Campus, was beyond fulfilling and rewarding. There are many more stories that I will share with you in my next Chicken Back Gravy Vol. 2 and my other books. But, looking back it is clear that had I received that scholarship, I would have been bonded to return to a company that would no longer suit me at the end of my BA (which I received with First Class Honours). Had I received that scholarship, I would have been on a different journey. One must always be BRAVE.

Several years later, one of my former male co-workers in that same Department recounted to me how EVERYONE watched to see what I would do. They

KNEW that I could not resign because of my personal and financial situation. They had all been talking about it. They watched me silently struggle with the decision. When I resigned it sent shock waves throughout my Department and others in the Company where my friends and colleagues were watching. In a Facebook discussion, years later, in 2017, that same former co-worker said to me:-

"Yes indeed, I know the struggles. From that day at Parkington when you decided to go back to school and the many challenges after. That's why I am so proud of you and your achievements. It was your movements that motivated me to go and do my degree at UTECH. I figured if you can, then I could also."

What I found out along the way is that you can inspire others to move beyond their Fear if you show them the way. People are always watching. They KNOW. Even if they do not say anything. They KNOW that you are facing a great FEAR. And they KNOW when you are being BRAVE against many odds.

Today, I tell people that "Sea Bottom People nuh Fraid ah Shark". Maybe you have heard me speak those words before, or, you have seen me write it somewhere. What I mean by this is that those who have risen from the depths have seen so many atrocities, so many strange and wonderful and terrifying creatures that a mere shark cannot strike fear in their hearts. *Chicken Back Gravy* people cannot be afraid of not having enough money to buy new clothes and shoes to model with others in the new wave of posing. Why would you? *Chicken Back Gravy* people have already been there and done that. So, if setting a goal or making a change in your life — for example, saving to get a down-payment on a house — means that you do not buy any new clothes for a year or two then how hard could that be? Your muscles have already been trained to do this.

A great quote on how to tackle fear, how to inject bravery into ourselves comes from one of my favourite genres, Science Fiction. This quote from *Dune* has also held me in great stead —

"I must not fear. Fear is the mind-killer. Fear is the little-death that brings total obliteration. I will face my fear. I will permit it to pass over me and through me. And when it has gone past I will turn the inner eye to see its path. Where the fear has gone there will be nothing. Only I will remain".

Hold fast to your dreams, and never let go. Breathe life into them. And when you are most paralyzed by fear of change, fear of the unknown and fear of what lies ahead, be BRAVE. *Chicken Back Gravy* people nuh watch nuh face.

Life Lesson #7
Pay Attention to your OWN Basket with your OWN Water — Focus Focus Focus

My madda ah nuh bank tella
Jahmiel, Things Take Time, 2016

If you have read carefully between all these lines you will realise there is another crucial life Lesson that I have been sharing all along. This Life Lesson #7 is that **You must pay attention to your OWN basket with your OWN water.** Everyone is carrying a different basket with different amounts of water. Yours is specific. You must focus on who you are, and what your specific journey is in order to achieve true success. You must understand your situation, your context and deal with these as personal specifics.

Here, the Who am I? mantra and exercise from Life Lesson #1 is critical. In order to understand your basket and the water you are carrying, you must know who you are. You must have answered the WHO AM I? question frankly and attained a critical level of self-knowledge. Each time you feel this slipping, you must go back and repeat this exercise.

Paying attention to your own basket with your own water will help you to refine your focus in a very clear and specific way. Ask yourself the following questions: How much water is in my basket? How heavy is it? What is the temperature of the water? What is the shape of my basket? Should I carry it on my back, on my hips, in my arms? In short, what is the sum total of all my achievements, my obstacles, the positives and negatives in my life at this moment? Once you have clarified this, not just who you are, but also what is your context and what are your positives and negatives at this time, then you can ask yourself other specific questions. These could include: Should I have two or three jobs? Should I go back to school part-time or full-time? Should I start a small business on the side? Should I buy a new car because everyone else is doing it? Should I leave this job and find another with better opportunities? Should I drop out of college and go start a small business? Should I migrate? Should I stay in my country? If I **don't do this now**, how will it impact my life in a year or two or three? On the other hand, **if I do this now**, how will it impact my life in a year or two or three? How will it impact my career or my personal goals? These are just some of the questions that you will want to ask yourself to ensure that you are making the right choices.

Nuh Fallah Hype (Don't Follow Hype)

Understanding the layout of your basket, your water, and how you should best carry it helps you to focus. This is another critical key to opening your door to success. The world we live in today is full of distractions, especially for poor, young people and not-so-young people, seeking to transform their lives. There are so many ads telling you that you will be like these wonderful, beautiful, happy people if you spend your hard-earned money on this deodorant, this soft drink, this car, this party, this outfit. Really. You will be encouraged by a variety of mechanisms to focus away from your goals. You will be promised instant rewards and lifelong success if you follow some fad, follow some hype. It is very easy to be distracted by hype in our social and traditional media cultures today. Hype is great when you are an artiste, plying your trade in popular cultures like dancehall and hip hop, or when you are in the film or media industry. Hype sells your products and attracts new customers when you are in the body beauty industry as a model, fashion designer, boutique owner, make-up artist, cosmetologist, plastic surgeon and so on. Hype sells your image. Hype is great when you are one of these new wave gurus selling your best life to others struggling in the depths. Hype sells your image. "Look at me! I am successful! See my wonderful life! Be like me!" Hype is not for you when you are struggling with limited resources to achieve your dreams. Nuh fallah hype as it can distract you, siphon away your limited resources of time, energy and money and result in higher levels of personal frustration and delay along your journey. Hype must always be avoided as it distracts you from the substance that is more valuable. I remember a little incident from several years ago that clearly illustrated the notion of hype over substance for a group of us.

StoryTime — Hype Over Substance

A group of us were annual attenders at Jamaica Carnival's annual Chukka Cove party event. That year, we drove into the venue and parked. A nice looking Honda car drove up and parked beside us. It had really great rims and a fabulous paint job. The six young men who came out of the vehicle were well decked out in the latest brand name jeans and shirts, with jewellery and brand name sneakers to match. Excitement! The driver of the car strutted proudly around his vehicle, making a big fuss and a lot of noise. Eventually we all went inside the venue, and, as was the usual, had a whale of a time wining and singing to the soca, calypso and dancehall tunes and enjoying the good vibes, great friends and flowing liquor.

Of course, we stayed until the end of "Chukka Cove" and so at just after 3.00am, we left the venue and went outside to the parking lot. Some persons had already left and others were leaving. When we reached to our car, we noticed a little gathering close by. It was the group of hyped, excited young men. This time, however, they were rallying anxiously around the car which had three flat tyres.

Three. The driver opened the trunk and eventually located his spare tire. The spare tire was also flat. By this time, a small crowd had gathered. Someone burst out laughing "All the spare tire flat!"

This true story of the very hype young men from Kingston stuck in St. Ann with the three flat tires and the spare that was also flat stayed with us for a while. We have no idea what happened and how they figured it out in the wee hours of the morning all the way in St. Ann. But we did try to figure out the message from that story. The message it left with me stayed and this is the same message I am reinforcing: Always ensure that you focus away from the hype. Focus on the substance. Keep your focus.

If you watch horses on the track on race days, some of them wear blinkers, that thing covering both sides of their faces. The blinkers narrow the horse's line of sight to a very singular focus on the track ahead. This keeps them focussed only on winning the race. Sometimes, as humans we need blinkers. Blinkers can include reducing your time on social media because you are being distracted by the often fabricated successful lives of your peers. Blinkers means removing yourself from attending too many parties where you must pretend to be "rich" and accomplished, even while you are struggling to achieve a financial or personal goal that you have been working towards for some time. Blinkers means finding and keeping company with individuals who are on the same journey as you at that time so that your mind is kept on track and you keep your focus. Avoid the hype. Focus on your success.

Understand Success for YOUR Basket with YOUR Water

Understanding your own basket and what is the volume and layout of your water also means that you will not be sucked into the foolishness about definitions of success that do not fit into your real life situation. A mantra that I have found to be very useful in my personal journey is this: **Success is never measured by what you have achieved, but rather by the depths from which you have climbed.** This means that you should not measure "success" based on the achievements of someone who simply had to reach out a hand across a table and take up their already packaged keys to success. No. You may not have it so easy. I am speaking about this because every Jamaican child is sold success stories that colour his or her generation. These success stories come from both inside our realities in our own country as well as from larger, more developed countries outside. In every single instance, every one of these "success" stories obscures the context of these "successful" men. And they are almost always men. So, success is usually gendered. Then, most of these "success" stories are about men who should be successful based on their starting point. Why not? They had the benefit of pre-packaged keys that opened the doors to already guaranteed opportunities for high levels of personal and financial success. Remember, they were already closer to or at the top of their societies. If they are in a classed society like Jamaica, then they usually emanate from the middle or upper classes. Or if they are in the USA they are usually white and many come from families that have higher incomes, parents with fantastic careers and hailing from suburban residential communities, with all the right social connections. Some have generations of financial legacies that they can draw upon. So, my generation learnt about men like the Matalons in Jamaica and Bill Gates in the USA. The current generation learns about Mark Zuckerberg of Facebook fame and many also learn about Jeff Bezos of Amazon fame. These stories obscure the social reality and accompanying privileges that provide a jump start. In the Jamaican context social class and skin colour and the legacies of networking by your parents and other family members translate into real social capital that guarantees greater access to the resources that make successful businessmen. In the USA it is exactly the same. Now, go look back at the Who Am I discussion in Life Lesson #1 and ask yourself those questions. And then examine YOUR Basket with YOUR Water.

Who is your Mother, your Father? This will play a key role in the opportunities you have. Do you have parents who work? Who have a salary from a job with a corporate entity? Who may have the benefits of health cards, pension plans, paid vacation leave? Some private and public sector entities provide assistance with educational expenses for minor children and also for university. Who AM I? Are you from a country designated as "developing" or "Third World"? Or are you an American? Do you live in the USA? Are you from the middle or upper classes? Ask yourself these questions. Are you a man? Are you a woman? Are you black? White? Too many stories obscure the social and economic privileges that often guarantee higher levels of social and economic success. Too many stories create false ideas in the minds of many *Chicken Back Gravy* children and young men and women about how they should dream. Too many stories suggest that every journey is the same and so all you have to do is BELIEVE. Too many stories claim that you do not need education because Gates and Zuckerberg had no college degree; even though the reality is that both men were in college when they decided on their respective moves which guaranteed their fortunes. They matriculated. They qualified. And what is the reality of the Jeff Bezos story? Did he start Amazon in his garage as a poor man? What social, educational and financial capital did he transfer into Amazon? I am not providing those answers here. This is why I insist that you must Read Read Read. And I don't mean the memes on social media or pre-digested effluent on someone's timeline. If you want to understand the success of these MEN go and read their biographies, go and read their stories — a great deal of useful information is online if you really want to find it. And a great deal is in books. When you read, ensure that you READ BETWEEN THE LINES. Could you take time off from your life, your college degree, your work to pursue your dream while being fully funded by your parents? Could you? Could you take an entire summer off while languishing in a wonderful mansion complete with pool so you and your friends could refine your idea into an innovative business? Could you? Do you have access to capital to start a business without paying any interest on it? Did the KFC Colonel begin frying chicken at retirement? Or was he engaging with this almost all his life? Go and READ. Read BETWEEN THE LINES.

When you have read and read between the lines, go back to Life Lesson #1 in this book and do the WHO AM I exercise again. WHO AM I? Who are you indeed? You are black. You are a man. Or you are a woman. You live in a different country from many of these men. A Third World country. A developing country with limited resources. You come from different communities. Most of us come from Ordinary people. My mother was a very Ordinary woman — a part-time domestic helper. Who IS your Mother? My father was absent. Sometimes your father is present but he cannot contribute much, because this is how it is for many people. Is/Was your Father present? Understand who YOU are. Then begin at YOUR beginning and DEAL with it. This is how you measure and guarantee true success. And this will help you to seek out and find your opportunities.

Opportunity Doesn't Always Knock

Opportunity a scarce, scarce commodity in these times
I say
Buju Banton, Untold Stories, 1995

My good friend Denise Black always said that Opportunity does not knock at the doors of some of us. It doesn't even pass by our lane or street or road. It doesn't even visit our community. NO. Indeed, the real truth is that for many *Chicken Back Gravy* people, opportunity will be passing by in another town miles away and you hear of it. So, you are at home in Linstead wondering where to find your Opportunity and you hear on the news, or see a post on social media that opportunity is passing by all the way in Montego Bay. Montego Bay is over two hours away (and sometimes up to almost 3 hours depending on the route you drive). What do you do? You must get up, go get a drive or take a bus to Montego Bay. Walk if you must. Beg or borrow the bus fare if you have to do so. But you must get up and rush out like a mad person. You don't even have any time to bathe properly or put on some decent clothing. You have to RUN. Falling down over yourself. Make yourself PRESENT and available in Montego Bay. And when you arrive at your destination and you see Opportunity, you have to rush in and grab Opportunity by the scruff of the neck, hit Opportunity over the head with something heavy, take it with you to the bus stop or taxi stand, or into the car that you have waiting, drive back home, and literally drag Opportunity to your doorstep. Recognize that this is a serious reality. This is the reality. You are locked in some inner city or poor community in urban or rural Jamaica or somewhere else that is definitely not on the "look good charts" of your society—waiting patiently for HELP. REALLY? You are locked somewhere where people like you and your family and friends and neighbours will be a statistic, a social negative, somewhere on some nice and decent bar graph or pie chart in some wonderful government institution or some local or international NGO. And you sit WAITING FOR OPPORTUNITY? Really? Wait forever maybe. Opportunity does not knock at your door. I am telling you that you must get up, go out and look it as we say in Jamaica. Go hustle it. Go and seek out YOUR Opportunity. Find it. Opportunities are everywhere. Just get up, change the perspective from which you see things and they become visible. Then, go after them, run, walk, crawl, beg a ride, do whatever works. But go after YOUR Opportunity.

The saying that "the fool stands in the middle of a river and dies of thirst" is very appropriate here. Rivers are full of water, but sometimes, if you are only waiting on nice, bottled water, or clean piped water, to come into your hands, you are going to die of thirst. Drink the damn river water. Lift up YOUR basket with YOUR water and go out and seek your Opportunity.

Life Lesson #8
Craft YOUR Roadmap
to Your Success

The worst ink survives the best memory, digital or otherwise
Donna P. Hope

The final Life Lesson that I will share with you is very simple. **Life Lesson #8 is Craft YOUR Roadmap to YOUR Success.** This means that you must have a plan. For everything. Achievement and success takes planning and time. Poor people are never successful overnight. That's called winning the lottery. A game of chance that you may never hit in your lifetime. Therefore, you must plan. And you must have a plan written somewhere.

Storytime — Write it Down

My good friend and colleague, Dr. Livingston White, shared something with me when we were undergraduates roaming the UWI's Mona Campus. This practice has proven to be a great tool in my life. It is very simple. He told me that he had read something somewhere that you must write out everything you plan to do each day –some small, some medium, some large. You must WRITE everything down on a list. Each time you complete a task, mark it off your list. Draw a line through it. We were sitting in the CARIMAC Lounge one afternoon, just hanging out and talking, between classes. "Write it down? I already do that." Do you mark them off when they are complete?" he asked. "You have to mark a line through them so that you acknowledge completion", he explained. I had never thought about that before. That day I learnt something new. The value of writing everything down. Of keeping a clear track of your daily plans and activities. And of your progress through each day. It sounds pretty simple, but it works. Each time you mark off something as complete, you are actually also marking something as achieved. I have been successfully using this tool ever since. I still use it every single day.

Interconnected Lists

I kept diaries as a child, the ones you write your little feelings in and talk about who you love and what you dream about. I have no idea where those diaries ended up with all the moving around that my family went through as a part of our *Chicken Back Gravy* journey. Then, I began keeping a journal in my early twenties and have continued to do so for several decades. I still do so. I have ALL my journals. I also learnt to keep diaries as a Legal and Confidential Secretary in the legal and corporate world. But it wasn't until Livingston shared that idea with me during our undergraduate years at the University that I began to put it into real practice. I WRITE everything down. Unlike many of my colleagues, friends and students, I still keep a large one-day-to-a-page diary, in line with my mantra "The worst ink survives the best memory, digital or otherwise". Having suffered the loss of my PDA and all the information stored in it at one point, I know this to be true. So, I write everything down that I plan to do each day. And then I work towards achieving every single one of them. In this age of smartphones, cloud and endless storage, I still keep a hardcopy backup. It has not failed me yet. But even more, the cognitive response towards the simple marking out each achieved task is palpable. You can literally FEEL yourself incrementally moving towards completion of larger tasks each time you mark out another small step along the way. Since every great move is really a series of interconnected small steps, you must WRITE OUT a variety of steps. It is true that the longest journey begins with a single step. But it is also true that the longest, hardest and most successful journey is made up of a whole lot of very very small, single steps.

You cannot depend on a simple daily list. If you are to plan your journey adequately, then you must have a series of interconnected lists. So, the daily list takes off from the monthly list of *Things-to-Do*. This list can be digital and acts as a kind of evolving master plan. So, for example, the items on my monthly list contribute to the items on the daily listings that are in my diary. The monthly *Things to Do List* contains larger monthly tasks that are unpacked daily. So, for example, I am to complete the process of writing *Chicken Back Gravy and Such Delights*, Volume 1. The monthly list will have two or three notations — (1) Write *Chicken Back Gravy*; (2) Complete *Chicken Back Gravy* Manuscript (3) Arrange graphics and layout for *Chicken Back Gravy*. The following month may already have a listing or two (1) Send *Chicken Back Gravy* for proofreading (2) Identify printer for *Chicken Back Gravy* and so on. A daily list that takes off from any of these could have (1) Call Printer on Spanish Town Road re CBG (2) Call Printer in New Kingston re CBG. (3) Call Tanya re proofreading CBG and so on. Then there is the MASTER OF ALL MASTER LISTS that no one ever sees — On it are things like WRITE FOUR MOTIVATIONAL BOOKS, PUBLISH POETRY BOOKS. Some of us also have a Bucket List of things to do or achieve, simply for fun or for some intrinsic reward. You would be surprised at how powerful these simple planning tools are in helping you to visualize what you want to do.

This kind of planning, where you WRITE EVERYTHING down is critical. What this helps you to do, based on your interconnected lists is to (1) Structure you activities on a daily, weekly, monthly and annual basis around your goals; (2) Engage in a clear pattern of incremental movement towards your achievements; (3) Track your progress on a daily, weekly, monthly and annual basis. Over time, you will be able to SEE the patterns in your routine and be able to plot the graph of your life. You will also be able to VISUALISE the progress that you have made and are making. This is very motivating.

Post-It Reminders

One other useful tip towards planning and visualising which I have found helpful is what I call the Post-It Reminders. I use different colours, sizes and shapes. But, if you have no Post-Its, any piece of paper, with a paper clip, piece of tape or even a piece of string will also work. If there is something that you MUST do or SHOULD do, but which you have been avoiding, then you must force your mind to process and acknowledge it so that you can move from thought to action. Write it in BIG, BOLD letters. If you have a marker, write it in BIG letters. RED letters are very useful. Then stick it on your mirror. Stick it on your fridge door. Stick it on the wall beside your bed so that when you open your eyes you will see it. Stick it on the inside of your front door so you MUST see it when you are about to open the door. This is a visual prod, like a kind of low level electrical shock that will force you to internalize and come to grips with this task you have to do or this thing you must complete. I also use it to REMIND me when I have something important to do. Sometimes I paste it over the front of my mobile phone and on the face of my laptop so when I open it in the mornings it is the first thing I see. I post notes in my purse. One must always keep on target. If you have an office at home or at work or both, paste it up in front of your desk so that you must see it. Put it on the windscreen of your car. Help yourself to help yourself. Once you see it, once it hits your line of vision, your mind begins to engage with it.

Today, there is a great deal of talk about Vision Boards. These usually come with pictures, nice things, well coined catchphrases and sayings etc. which are tools that we are told must guarantee success. Many workshops now use these, and everyone leaves feeling great! Time to achieve! This is a great start. But, simply visualising your dreams will not move you from your *Chicken Back Gravy* status. Every idea that is put into a visual must also be put into active reality. As I said in Life Lesson #5, you will have to WORK. And *Chicken Back Gravy* people always have to work Harder and Smarter in order to achieve their dreams.

Dream Big and Write Them On Paper

In all that I have said remember this even as you begin to sketch your interconnected plans—DREAM BIG, GIGANTIC..BIGGER THAN THE LITTLE CAGE RESERVED FOR YOU AND YOURS. AND BREATHE LIFE INTO YOUR DREAMS TO MAKE THEM FLY—IT WORKS. Plan everything. Write your dreams down. Then break down those dreams into tangible steps over a period of months, weeks and days.

Do you remember that exercise you used to be given in Primary or Prep School? It was a mini-essay called "Myself in Ten Years' Time". Most Jamaican children have had to write a version of this at some point in their lives. Do you remember any of the dreams that you wrote down as plans in those essays as a child? How many of those plans did you achieve? Do you still have dreams? Have you ever written them down? If not, now is the time. Get a piece of paper, get a writing pad, get a book and WRITE DOWN YOUR DREAMS IN HARDCOPY. Look at them. Read them over at nights before you go to sleep. Read them first thing in the morning when you wake up.

You will be the only person responsible for your OWN dreams. If you plan to go back to school, you must begin to look at programs of study. You must begin to look at funding options. Maybe you can get a Students Loan from the Students Loan Bureau. Or maybe you qualify for a scholarship as a child of an employee or as an employee of a particular entity? Apply for the loan. Apply for the scholarship. APPLY to go back to school. Write it down and then go and do it. If you plan to own a home, maybe the National Housing Trust with its cheap loans earned at the expense of PAYE workers should be among your first options? Go on the National Housing Trust's website and see. Call their Customer Care Department. Get the necessary information. WRITE IT DOWN. Start looking at Houses for Sale in the Classifieds. Then put your plan into action and seize the opportunities. NO one is going to fund your dreams. And NO ONE is going to get up, plan them and achieve them on your behalf.

Always dare to dream. And then put your plans on paper. But do not leave them there. Put your plans into action. Always take that first step towards moving from *Chicken Back Gravy* to something more delightful.

AFTERTHOUGHTS

The full has never been told.
Buju Banton, Untold Stories, 1995

When it is over and done, and you look back, you must be able to say, "I did my best". "I tried". "I did not give up". And you will be satisfied.

These words on paper from me to you are just one more tool to help you to do just that. I can say with supreme confidence that I did my best. Against insurmountable odds. I did my utmost best as Mama used to say. And I survived. I gambled and took extreme risks and won handsomely. *Chicken Back Gravy* is always an option in my life. "Remember who you ARE". I am still that girlchild from Linstead. But I am also many more things. This first volume of my *Chicken Back Gravy and Such Delights* journey has helped me, in many ways, to Remember who I AM.

I would be telling a lie if I said that sitting at my desk in front of my laptop and writing these words has been easy. No. But this is one first part of the story, my story that I know has great value to you and everyone else who has read it. There is a great deal more that I will share with you from my multi-faceted life journey. This is but the first of many parts. My greatest Hope is that you have been inspired enough by my *Chicken Back Gravy* story to move ahead with some dream of yours.

Until we meet again, I wish you wonders, marvels and every success as you move along your life journey.

Love and Blessings
Professor Donna P. Hope
January 2019